The Definitive Guide to the

1-1-3 Match-up Zone

By Jason Montgomery

ISBN: 978-0-6151-4378-1

Published 2007 by Jason Montgomery

First Edition

CONTENTS

Introduction

In the spring of 2001 we had just completed our first season as a coaching staff at Saint Catharine College in central Kentucky. As part of our annual review we met as a staff to look at what went well and what didn't from the previous season. One important part of the review process was taking a look at our opponents and especially those that finished at the top of the heap in our conference. That particular season Chattanooga State had run through our conference with relative ease and finished a solid 7th at the NJCAA national championships. As we began to evaluate Chattanooga and what set them apart we found a team that was talented but not to the point of explaining their dominance of the league. The only characteristic we could find was the apparent difficulty other schools had in dealing with Chattanooga's match-up zone.

I must confess that we too had some real issues in dealing with the match-up. And even today after nearly fifteen seasons of coaching, I could probably count on both hands the number of times that we faced other teams that played a true match-up zone. I believe that the rarity of facing this defense, as well as the characteristics of the defense itself, makes it so hard to attack.

It was in response to Chattanooga's defensive system, that we made the decision to put a match-up zone in ourselves. At that time I was a man-to-man purest that believed in dictating the game to our opponents on both ends of the floor. We were consistently in the top fifteen in the nation in team offense and played zone only when we had a huge lead or crippling foul trouble. Our philosophy had not changed and we intended the match-up to be our last ditch zone option. The added benefit that we hoped for was that we would be able to work against the very defense that we would need to defeat to have a shot at winning the league.

We began the process of gathering information from a slew of sources on match-up zones. This was a defense I had never taught and was definitely pulling me out of my comfort zone. I was amazed on how many sources that claimed to be a match-up were just glorified versions of regular zone defenses. We finally settled and based our system on Lute Olsen's 1-2-2 / 2-3 Arizona match-up and so began what would become a career changing experiment.

We began the season still in the mindset of being a man-to-man team and riding the wave of a great recruiting class. As fate would have it we got in early foul trouble in our second game of the season and for the fist time we went into our match-up. Not only did we prevent our foul issues from worsening, we caused some real problems for our opponent. Over the next few games we found ourselves going more and more to the zone and by seasons end we were a 90% or more zone team. As the season progressed we refined our system, created some new drills and created unique trap opportunities. This evolution continues to today and has remarkably allowed us to post 129 wins over the past six seasons and during the remainder of my stay at SCC we continued to post impressive offensive numbers including a school record single game total of 137 points.

In the course of this book I will introduce the 1-1-3 and several variations as well as trapping and press options. In addition to the defense itself we will also look at different common attacks you will face as well as what I feel are the best ways to attack a match-up. I truly believe that this is the most comprehensive look at the 1-1-3 you can find. I hope you enjoy.

What sets the match-up apart?

There are several characteristics and considerations that are worthy of note when looking at the match-up zone and making the decision on whether to implement the defense. One of the most common cited advantages is the mix of man and zone characteristics. In a true match-up zone, a player with the ball in your respective zone becomes your man and is played as such while the zone provides your help side defense. Another huge advantage of a true match-up is its versatility. If you are a small team you have the ability front and double larger post or if you are blessed with good post size you can keep your big player inside while applying pressure on the perimeter.

As with all zone defenses there are some weaknesses that you must take in consideration. Since the match-up combines both man and zone principles this will affect practice time. It is essential that you spend time working on man techniques such as help side and one on one defensive skills. In addition, communication is paramount due to the rotations dictated by the defense, which when they break down can allow wide-open looks.

All these factors along with what you are looking to accomplish on the defensive end of the floor must be taken into consideration when deciding to implement the match-up zone. Our philosophy has, and will always be, to dictate the tempo of the game through our defense. We always work extremely hard to keep the ball out of the paint and allow only contested three point shots.

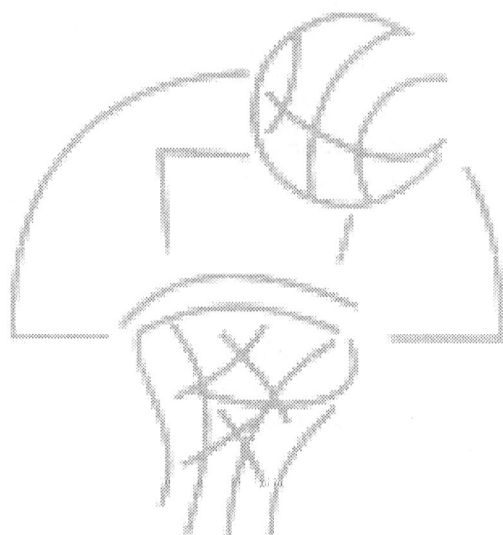

Terminology

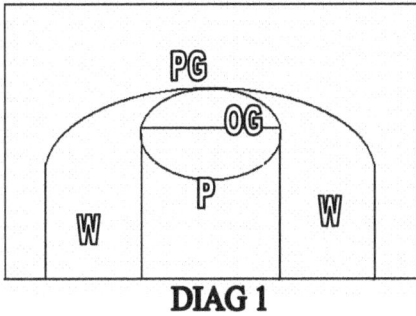

DIAG 1

In the 1-1-3 there are two distinct units that must be understood independent of the defense as a whole. The first of these groups is comprised of the two guards who form what we will refer to as the tandem. The top guard in the tandem is referred to as the point guard (PG) with the second guard referred to as the off guard (OG). The second unit in the zone is comprised of the wings (W) and the post (P). This group is what we will call the base **(DIAG 1)**. As you will see later these two groups must work both independent and together to allow the defense to be successful.

Player Responsibilities

The first and most important fundamental rule that must be taught in introducing the match-up is the concept of "reading down". By this we mean that the point will make the initial defensive decision and that decision then tells the off guard where to play, that read then dictates to the wings their position and ends with the post alignment being determined by the play of the wings. I cannot impress how important it is for players to trust their reads and fulfill their responsibility. **The quickest way for the defense to completely breakdown is by players attempting to cover for someone else's mistake. When this takes place in a defense that is this interdependent you will quickly find the defense in complete and total breakdown.**

With the importance of reading down understood, it is now time to learn the basic responsibilities of each position.

Point Guard (PG) -   The point guard should pick up the ball-handler a dribble or two across half court, (remember that you have man responsibility and can not allow yourself to be beaten off the dribble so apply your pressure appropriately), the primary objective is now to force the ball-handler to commit to one side of the floor. Pushing the ball-handler to a side allows for several advantages including allowing the defense to be more aggressive and limiting the options and passing angles of the offense.

Off Guard (OG)-   The primary responsibility of the off guard is to protect the high post. In the event that the high post is unoccupied the OG will then pick a side of the floor and position himself or herself so that they will take the first pass to that wing. The OG should always match out to the side of the opponent's primary shooter when possible. When matching out the OG should never widen out wider than the elbow as to always be in a position to cover the high post.

High Post Open

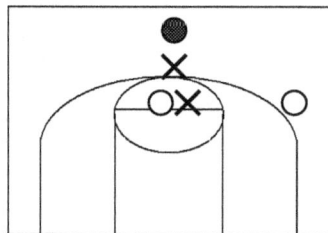

High Post Open Occupied

<u>Wings (W)</u>-

Primary responsibility for the wing players is defending the offense's first pass to the wing as well as skip passes. In teaching the defense to close out the offensive player it is important to stress two areas. First, it is key that the defense allows as little penetration as possible; therefore the defender must stay low and look to contest the shot while playing the drive first. While closing out we teach that the defender closes out to the baseline side with the left hand up and the butt low. This is taught this way as most shooters are right handed and should be contested with the left hand and by attacking the baseline shoulder we force the offensive player to drive middle where we have both maximum help and allows for the easiest defensive rotation.

<u>Post (P)</u>-

The responsibility of the post is to front the ball side post player and to play the first baseline pass from a player defended by the wing. The post should work an arc from block to mid-post to block to better allow them to front ball side and prevent the defense from pinning (DIAG 2). We will in later sections discuss the option of playing a big post behind inside.

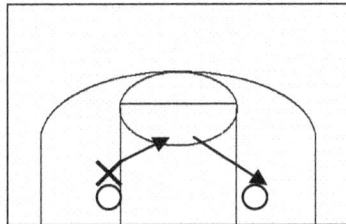

DIAG 2

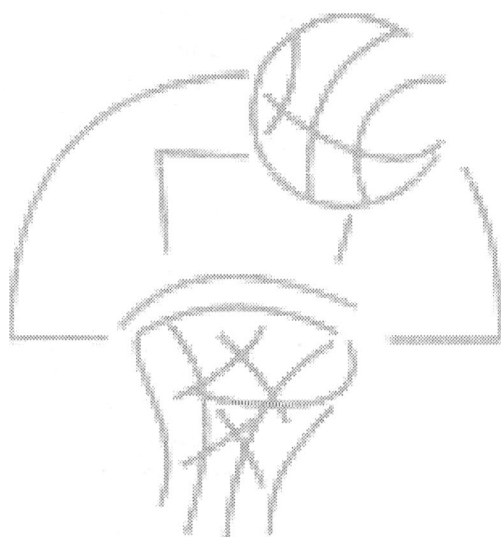

Basic Rotation

As discussed earlier the 1-1-3 is predicated on the premise that all players must "read down" from the initial decisions of the guards in the tandem. Before getting in to the more complex rotation principles we will show in diagrams 3 and 4 the responsibilities of all players when the ball is at the top. For a point of reference in our discussion of rotation we will go through the rotation progressions using both the 3-2 and 1-3-1 offensive sets. It is also important at this time to point out the importance of the initial starting positions of players in the base as you will notice the post will always arc into the mid post when the ball is up top and the wings must always be outside any players form the blocks out to short corner. In diagram 3 we see the offense in a 3-2 look with no player in the high post. In this instance the off guard will declare a side of the floor by shifting to that elbow. This read now tells the wing opposite the OG that they will have first pass to the wing while the OG will take the pass to their side. The post will work their arc fronting the ball side post. In DIAG 4 we see the offense in a high / low or 1-3-1 set. This is one of the most common seen sets to attack the match-up as it is often mistaken for a 2-3 zone. In this case the OG will take the high post. This read now tells the wings that the will have the first pass to both wings. The post again will work their arc.

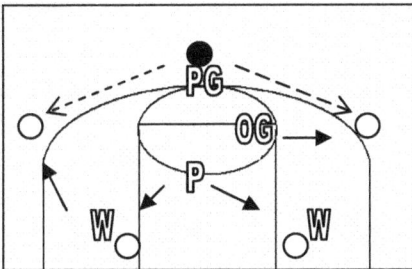

DIAG 3

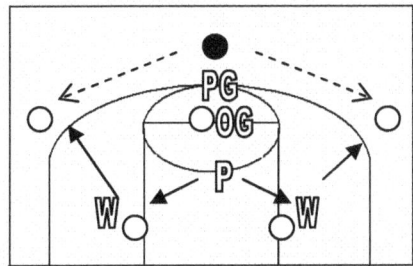

DIAG 4

Defending the pass to the wing.

Once the pass is made to the wing there are several considerations that need to be made. First, I will discuss some strategies common to all situations regardless of the offensive set. As you will see in diagrams 5, 6 and 7 the backside wing should always play up the lane but never deeper than with one foot in the lane. Though the backside wing must provide help-side to the post, (as you remember the post is always working to front their man), it is absolutely essential for the backside wing to not play flat or too deep in the lane. When this happens the defense is now susceptible to flashes to the mid post as well as shooters drifting into the slot. When the defense plays up the lane shooters must stay wider to receive skip passes, (great opportunity for a steal), and flashes are far easier to see and bump all while maintaining a position to help on all lobs to the post. In diagram 5 you will again see a high open post. As the ball goes to the wing to the side that the OG has already declared by their shift, the OG will then take the first pass to this side. In this case the zone plays very much like a traditional 2-3 with the PG dropping to cover the high post and the base defending the drive and entry passes to the post. In diagram 6 you will see a pass opposite the OG in this case the W takes the first pass with the PG and OG remaining in their current positions. The wing taking the first pass now tells our post that they will now have any pass to the baseline side of the wing. Diagram 7 shows our pass to a wing with an offensive player in the high post. In this situation the wings will take the first pass to either wing and the PG and OG will remain at home.

Open High Post (OG side)

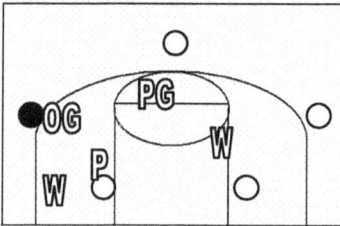

DIAG 5

Open High (opp. OG side)

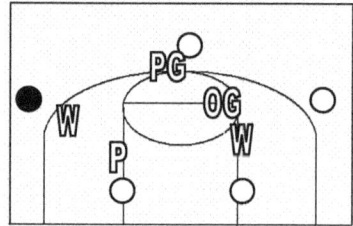

DIAG 6

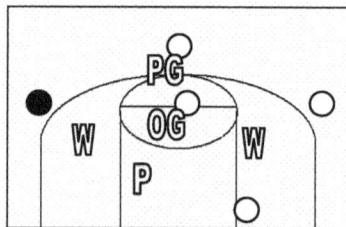

DIAG 7

Defending the pass to the baseline.

       This is the situation that sets the match-up apart from other zone defenses. As with the pass to the wing, we have a couple of guidelines that will apply regardless of the offensive set. The most important of these principles is denial of ball reversal on all passes to the deep corner. As you will see in each of the following three diagrams when the ball is in the corner the ball side guard will deny the first pass out. In diagram 8 we again see an open high post and the offense has stepped the ball side post out to the deep corner. As with a pass to the OG side of the floor the defense plays much as a 2-3 zone would with the W taking the pass. Please note the OG stays out to deny the easy reversal and the backside W is up the lane providing help side as well as sitting on the skip pass. In a situation where the W has taken the pass to the wing, (diagrams 9 and 10), we have a unique situation that allows the match-up the versatility to work against any set. In this case the W playing the ball conveys information to both the post, wing and in this case the point guard. Any pass to the baseline will be covered by the Post, the W must then drop and cover the post while the PG will shift to deny the first pass out. This rotation we call the <u>post slide</u>. This is both the single most difficult rotation to master as well at the most important. Failure to rotate properly will allow for the offense to find a wide-open shot. Note that in diagram 10 the OG does not leave to cover as the rule is that you never leave the high post.

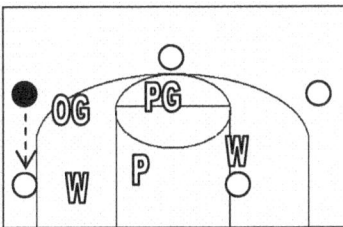

DIAG 8

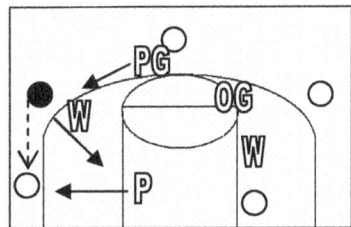

DIAG 9

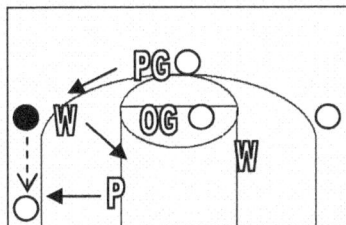

DIAG 10

Depending on your personnel you have one of two choices following a post slide. First, if you are comfortable with your personnel and have no true center no further adjustments will be necessary. All that has happened is your ball side wing and post have now switched positions. If you have a true center or a player that you wish to keep in the lane you can now do what we call a post interchange. On the first pass back out of the corner the W and P simply return to their original positions.

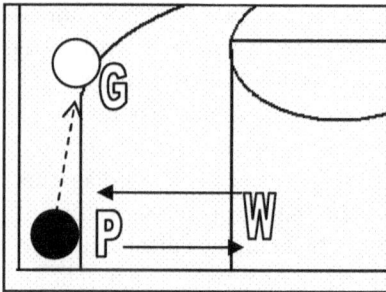

POST INTERCHANGE

DIAG 11

Exceptions to never leaving the high post.

Now that you have a feel for the basic rotation of the zone I want to point out two situations where it is necessary to break the cardinal rule of never leaving the high post.

1) The Two-Guard Front – When teams attack the zone with a two guard front and place someone in the high post this puts tremendous pressure on the defensive guards. In most situations where the point plays the ball and the off guard is defending the high post the wing would be responsible for the first pass. In the case of a 2-1-2 set this creates a situation where the coverage for the wing is simply physically not possible. To combat this problem the guards in the tandem must do what we call "playing two". Here we simply interchange coverage of the high post on the pass. Key in this interchange is the ability of the guard to play in the space between the high post and the ball until the backside guard can cover the high post

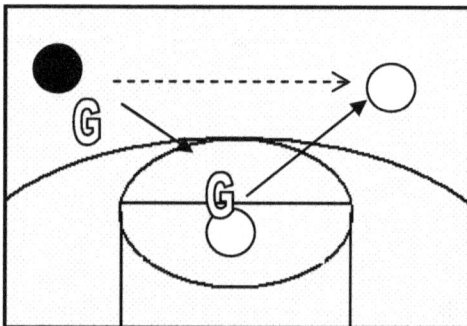

thus allowing the ball side defender to apply ball pressure. In this situation the defender will play at the halfway point between the high post and the perimeter player – close enough to the guard to contest a shot while playing close enough to the high post to prevent the entry pass.

2) One Guard Front Ball Reversal With Occupied Hi Post– In the case of a team playing a 3-2 or a 1-3-1 offensive set and the ball reaches the deep corner while the high post is occupied, the reversal may create a situation where the tandem must again "play two". As we see in the diagram, as the ball is passed from the wing to the point the P must leave the high post, ("play two"), as the OG comes to cover the high post. From this point wings will now take all passes to the wing.

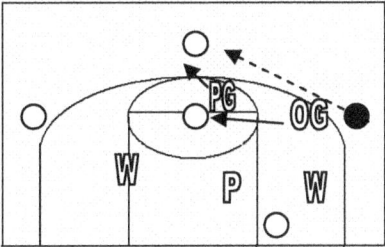

DIAG 13

Defending the baseline drive.

Even though we stress that our wings push the ball toward the middle there will be times when an offensive player drives baseline. In this case the post will step up to take the drive as the wing doubles down. As the post leaves to take the drive the backside wing must step over and take the ball side block. This exposes the backside block and forces the guard in the high post, in this case the OG, to drop and cove the backside while the other guard covers the high post. (DIAG 14).

As the offense passes out from the drive the defense will then match back out (DIAG 15).

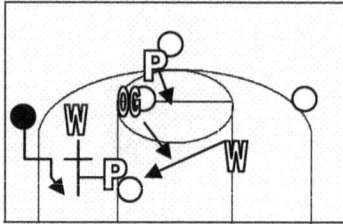

DIAG 14

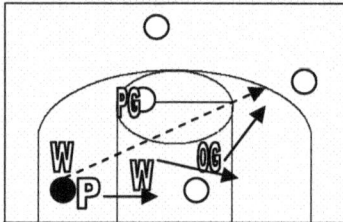

DIAG 15

Bump Option

Another option that is available to the defense is what we call the "bump option". In a situation where an offense will run a shooter along the baseline from deep corner to deep corner the defense can some times be slow on defending the corner on ball reversal. In this case we simply push or "bump" our wing off of the first pass. This allows the wing to now cover the deep corner much as a 2-3 would play. Diagrams 16 - 18 show this option versus the baseline runner.

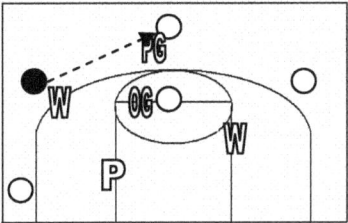

DIAG 16

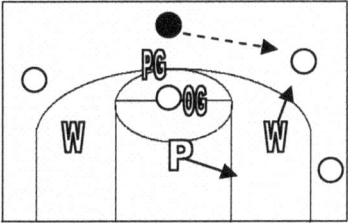

DIAG 17

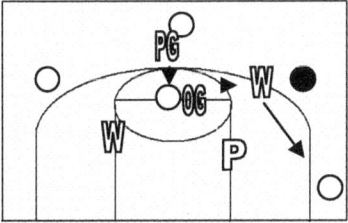

DIAG 18

Breakdown Drills

Let me begin the breakdown portion by again stressing the importance of man-to-man principals. Since each player will be one on one or providing help side defense these basics are key to the defense's success. Below is a brief overview of the drills we use to teach these principals.

Shell (4 on 4 and 5 on 5)

In our man defense we follow four rules. 1) We always play "up the line" between the ball and our man with a hand and foot in the passing lane (diagram below). 2) We always play with our belly facing our man. This is a cardinal rule as when we turn our backs to the offense we allow cuts. 3) We never allow a cutter to cut between the ball and the defender. 4) Body contact is ALWAYS to the offense's advantage. This will be explained more in the section devoted to attacking the defense but for now we begin teaching this concept in man principals as we want to beat the offense to position and not allow our players to be bumped, screened or pinned in the post.

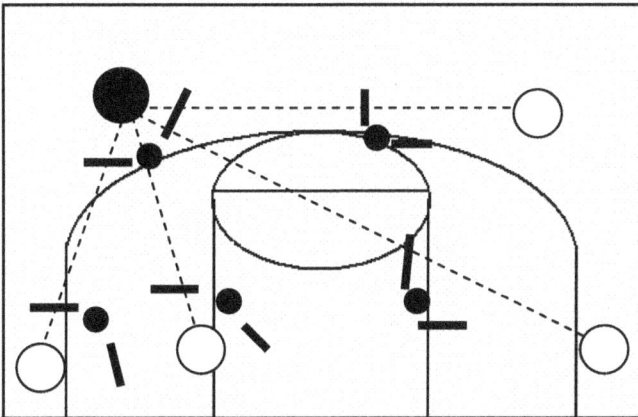

DIAG 19

Diagram 19 shows proper defensive position with defenders up the line, belly to their man and a hand and foot in the passing lanes. When teaching man to man we do several one on one drills. In each drill we stress proper stance, movement such as slides and drop steps.

Closeout and Contest Drill:

This is a drill that can be varied to fit what you want to accomplish on the perimeter of the zone. If you are a team that desires to be a little more conservative and deny all penetration then in the drill you will want to stress staying low with a hand up to contest and getting a good block-out. We choose to be a little more aggressive from time to time. In our system we want to make it a point to not allow shooters to catch and shoot. We stress disrupting offensive rhythm of the offensive players we feel may be threats from behind the arc. Part of our philosophy entails sometimes actually flying by shooters and forcing the drive trusting our backside rotation to defend the drive. In this drill we place shooters in both deep corners with our defenders in a line under the basket. The coach is at the top of the key with the ball and begins the drill by having the defender chop their feet. The coach will pass to one of the shooters and the defender must close out and contest the shot. We will do two variations on this drill. In the first variation shooters always shoot the shot and defenders always overrun the shooter and then recover back to go for the rebound. In variation two we assume we are closing out a drive threat. In this scenario we close out to take away the drive first while still getting the hand up on the shooter. The offensive player in this situation may shoot or drive. We spend a great amount of time on this drill trying to focus our players on closing out hard but not over compensating on any shot fakes.

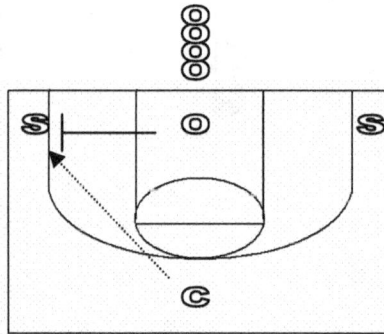

DIAG 20

Contest Drill

Closeout 1 on 1 Drill

This is another variation of the closeout drill that incorporates two added dimensions needed to play an effective match-up – one on one ball defense and blocking out. In this drill the coach passes to an offensive player at the top of the key who is closed out by the defender coming from under the basket. The offensive player may shoot or drive but are limited to three dribbles. The defender must closeout, defend the drive, "belly up" to the shooter when they pick up the dribble and box out.

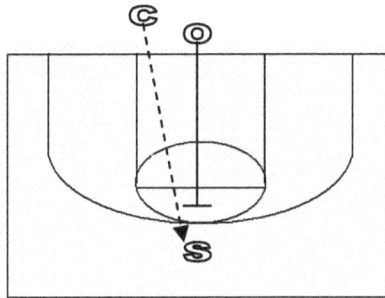

DIAG 21

Full Court 1 on 1

Another mainstay of man drills. Players are in pairs and will work to turn the offensive player at ½ speed to mid-court then play live one on one to the goal. Again as in the drills we stress containing the drive, contesting the shot and boxing out.

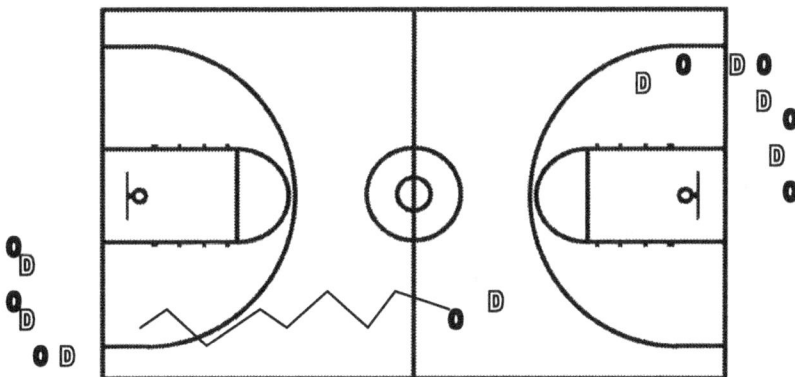

DIAG 22

Now that a team has a firm grip of the man to man principals necessary to be successful in the match-up we can move to the drills that help reinforce the rotations of the defense. We use two variations of the same basic drill to teach the rotation of the guards in the tandem. In diagrams 23-24 we see the offense in a three guard look, (point and two wings) and an open high post. We allow the three offensive players and the defensive players work on their rotation.

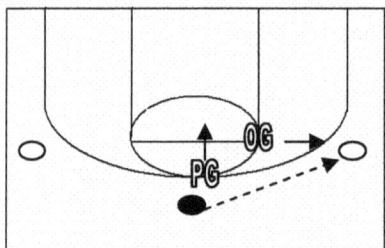

DIAG 23

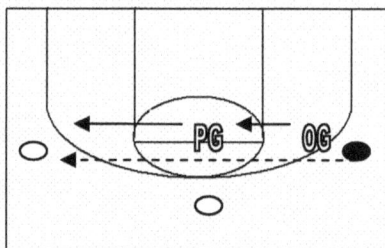

DIAG 24

In diagram 23 we see the pass go to the wing on the side that the OG was shading, (remember by picking a side in an open high post offense the OG is telling the wings if they will have the first pass or not), and the OG takes the pass. As this happens the PG drops and covers the high post. If the pass were reversed the PG and OG would match back out. In DIAG 24 we see a skip pass. Even though it is the primary responsibility of the wing to cover skip passes there are times when a guard must take this pass such as when there is a backside screen. In this case the PG must hold in the high post as the OG drops to cover allowing the PG to match out.

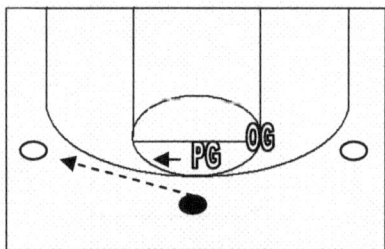

DIAG 25

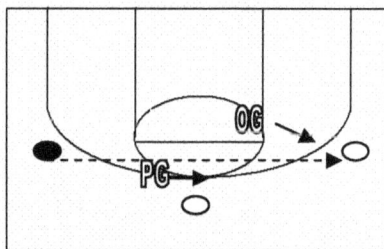

DIAG 26

Diagrams 25 and 26 show the same offensive alignment only now we see the initial pass going opposite the OG designated side. With no base – the tandem guards must know that this pass belongs to the wing and play as such. In this case the PG would only shift to the ball side while the OG maintains the high post. Diagram 26 shows the skip coverage just as we saw in diagram 24.

In the case of the same three guard set with the addition of a player in the high post the rotation changes. In diagram 27 if a pass goes to either wing both the PG and OG will stay at home as with a player in the high post first pass will always be the responsibility of the wing. We again work to cover the skip as in DIAG 28. In the case of a skip with an occupied high post the OG will leave to cover out but only after the PG has dropped to cover the high post.

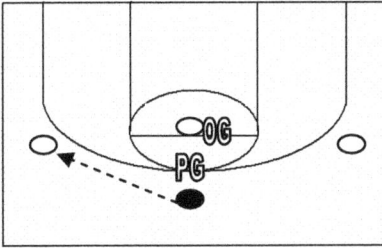

DIAG 27

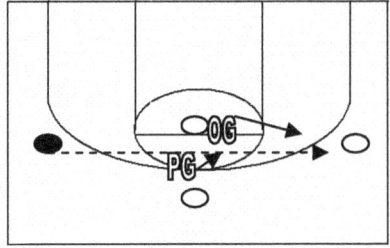

DIAG 28

A second variation of this drill deals with the other of the most common attacks that many teams use versus the 1-1-3. In this variation we place our offensive players in a two guard front with an occupied high post. This allows us to work on the concept of "playing two" that we discussed earlier. As the pass goes from guard to guard the PG and OG must allow the other defender to cover down to the high post before matching out. Diagram 29 shows this rotation while diagram 30 proper defensive position a player must have as they await help allowing them to leave the high post, (playing two).

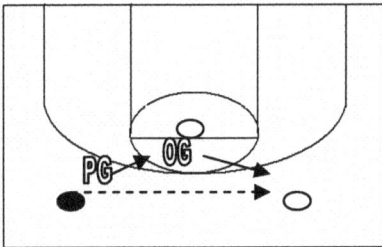

DIAG 29

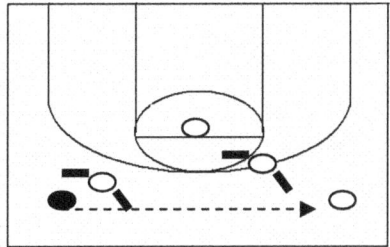

DIAG 30

** Note in diagram 30 that the defender attempts to occupy as much space as possible, splitting the difference close enough to contest a perimeter shot while playing the passing lane in order to defend the high post.

We will now show how we work our fundamental rotation for our base. Again in this set of drills we use two variations. In our first variation we place our offense in a 5 out set. Defensively we use our only our three base players. For the sake of rotation we assume that the high post is occupied so that the wing will take all first passes. This forces the defense to utilize the post slide to cover the corner and allows us to work on rotating back as the ball is passed back from the corner to the wing.

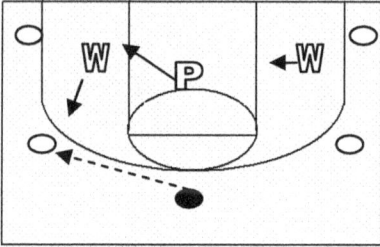

DIAG 31

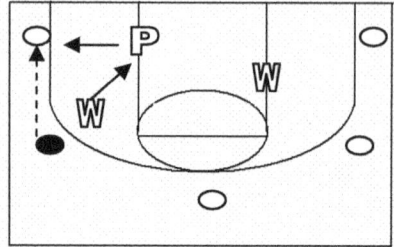

DIAG 32

* Note in diagram 32 that the backside wing is positioned up the lane to provide post help as well as cover the skip pass.

In our second variation we add two players in the low post. This again allows us to work on our rotation but adds the dimension of forcing the post to work the arc from block to block in order to gain the necessary fronting position.

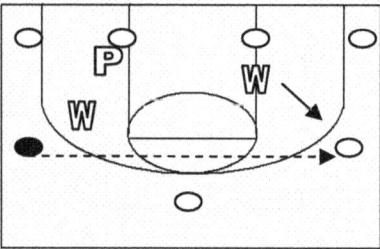

DIAG 33

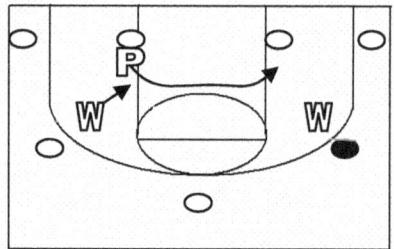

DIAG 34

Keys in teaching base rotation are:

1. Post players must always work an arc in order to maintain proper position and not get pinned.

2. Post and wing must think one pass ahead at all time in order to cover the post slide on passes to the corner.

Team Drills

A final variation of this drill pits eight offensive players vs. the five defenders in the match-up. This drill marks the culmination of teaching this defense. In this drill we attempt to put maximum pressure on the defensive unit by forcing the team to cover all areas – low post and high post as well as post slides.

DIAG 35

In diagram 35 we see the initial starting position for this drill. With the high post occupied wings will take all fist passes. It is important in this drill to stress three points; proper backside position for the wings, the post working the arc in order not to get sealed on ball reversal and guard rotation in the post slide to cover the pass out of the deep corner. In diagrams 36-38 we see a sample of the rotations in this drill.

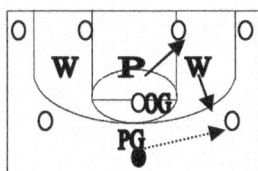 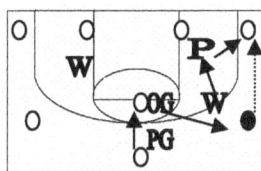 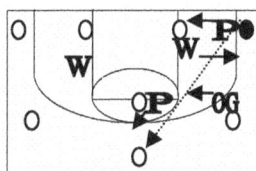

DIAG 36   **DIAG 37**   **DIAG 38**

This may be the most complete way to reinforce and teach the overall rotation responsibilities as failures will become glaringly obvious. As your team becomes more comfortable with the defense you can use several different variations on this drill. We have found that by using seven offensive players, (one less low post), and allowing the offense to move at will is especially difficult. A new area of concern emerges with this variation and that is communication. With only seven offensive players you can now use an open post or have players flash high. In both cases this forces players to change rotations, communicate and read down from the point to the post. I would encourage you to play with this drill as the more complex situations your team can accommodate the easier the defense becomes with only five players.

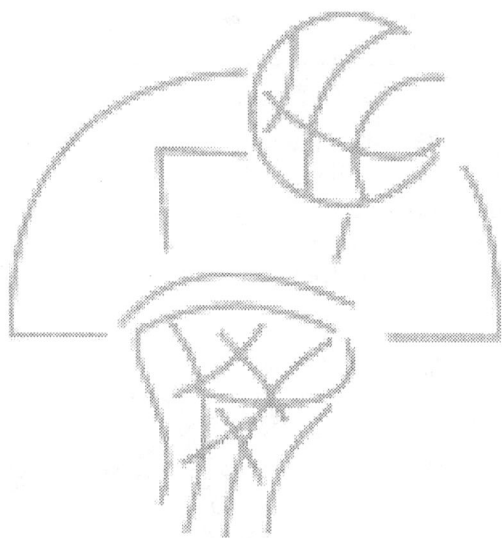

Trap Variations

1-1-3 ¾ court trap

This defensive look begins by extending the defense to a ¾ court look. The point will pick up the players in the backcourt around the 3 point line. The second guard is positioned around mid court with the base players located around the free throw line extended, (see diagram 39).

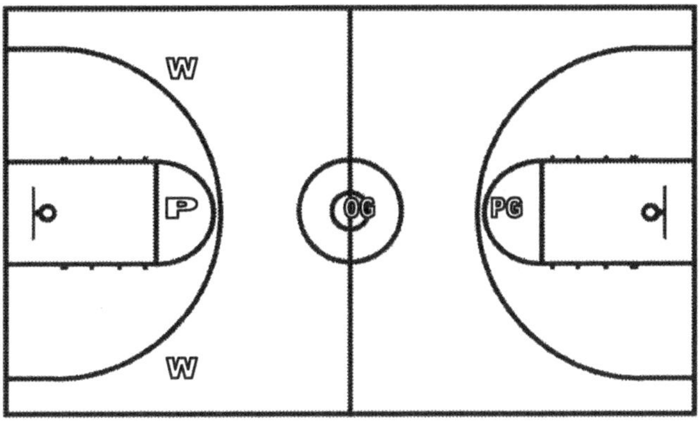

DIAG 39

Trap off the dribble across half court

The basic rotation of the 1-1-3 ¾ is the same as the half court match-up. As the offensive player gets closer to half court the PG will close down space on the offensive player. The OG will have the responsibility of taking the first pass out of the trap to the middle. Ball side wing will trap with the PG. The post will take the first pass sideline out of the trap. Backside wing will initially drop to prevent the offense to throw over the top and as the trap takes place the backside wing will take the middle of the floor.

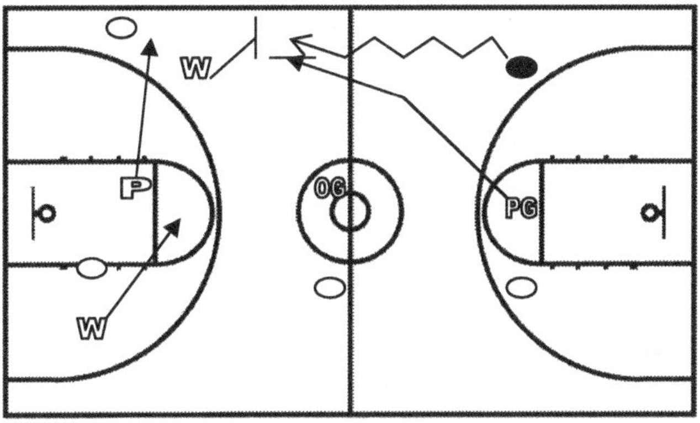

DIAG 40

Trap off the reverse

One common tactic teams will use to attack this defense is to drive to near ½ court and throw the skip. In this case the OG will leave and trap while the PG takes the reverse, (DIAG 41).

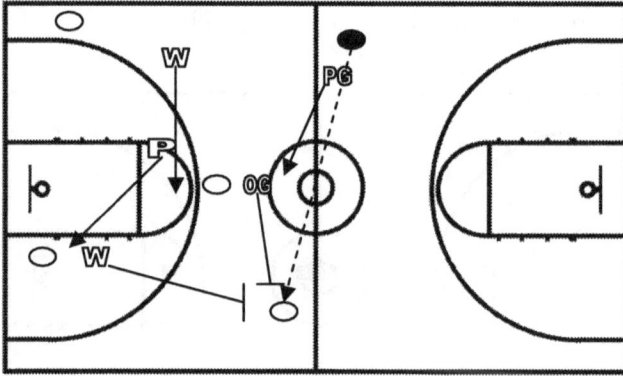

DIAG 41

In any situation where the offensive team breaks the trap the team falls back into the ½ court match-up. In the following two diagrams I will show two common looks the offense will use that causes the defense problems. The first situation is the overload in the middle. In this situation the offense places two players in the middle of the floor causing the defense to have problems reading who to cover. In this scenario the defender must work with the post prior to the trap and the backside wing after the trap to take this away. Always remember the when in doubt the off guard will take the first pass out of the trap, (DIAG 42).

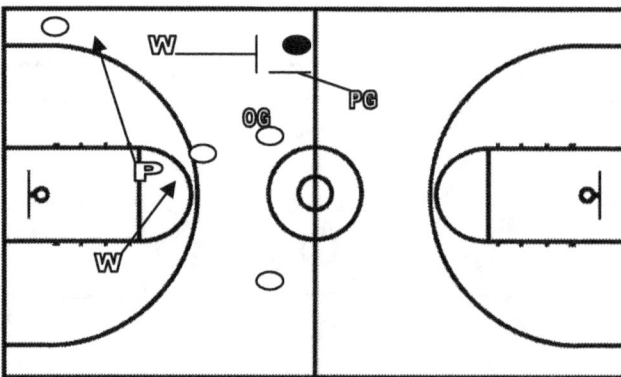

DIAG 42

A second set that may cause defensive problems is the overload of the sideline. In this scenario the offensive team will attempt to place two players down the sideline and catch the defense in rotation and throw over the trap. This exposes a huge key to the success of this defense – allowing the trap to come to the wing. We never allow the wing to attack the trap rather it is the job of the guards to force the ball to the wing for the trap. Note that if two players are on the wing we will always play behind first player. This is done to allow the trap in the event the offensive player passes up the floor.

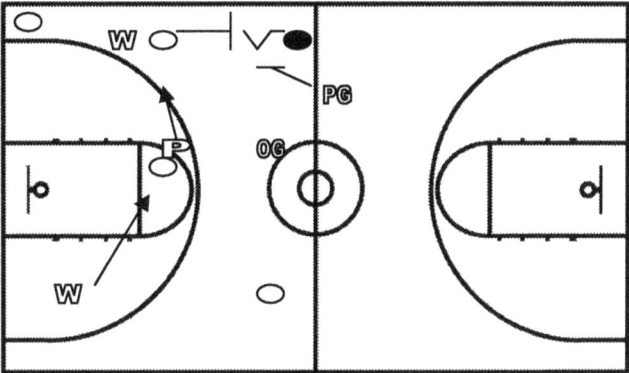

DIAG 43

The final situation that must be taught is the concept of staying with the trap. In the event that two players attempt a trap they will continue the trap until that player passes. In diagram 44 we see where the offensive player eludes the trap and continues along the sideline. We stay with the trap and eventually get it in the deep corner. In any case like this the other defenders must adjust their position to compensate.

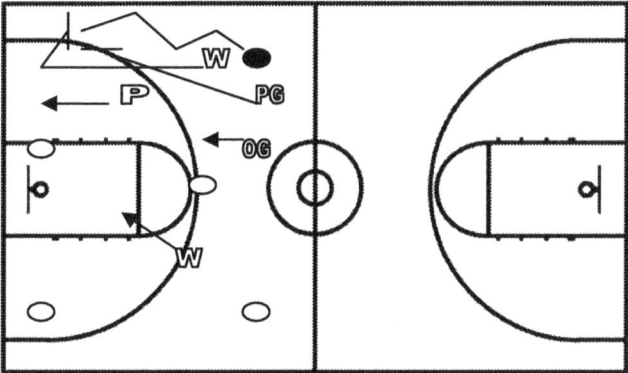

DIAG 44

Half Court Point Trap

In this option we show what looks like our normal half court look but use the tandem guards to trap at mid court as the ball crosses the time line. Here the PG and OG will jump the ball handler as the wings take first pass out and the post takes the high post. The action is keyed by a verbal call from the point guard. This is a high risk high reward look and if your wings are slow at all in taking away the wing pass the offense will get a very good offensive look.

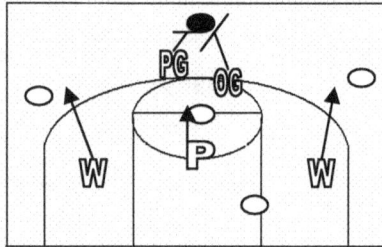

DIAG 45

Half Court Wing Trap

In this look we trap the first pass to the wing. Here the PG follows the pass and traps. The Post will take the first pass sideline and the OG will take the reverse while the backside wing takes the high post leaving the skip open.

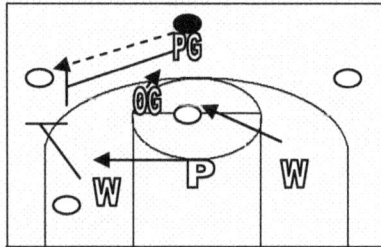

DIAG 46

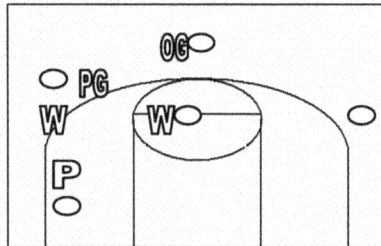

DIAG 47

In this option we look to take advantage of the offense attempting to make us rotate by going to the deep corner. In this look we trap with the wing and the post on the pass down. One tandem guard will take away the first pass out while the other takes high post. The backside wing must take away the low post.

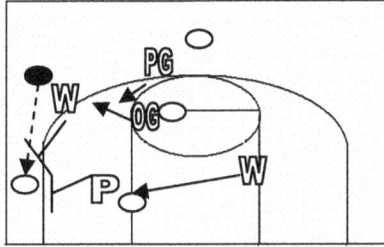

DIAG 48

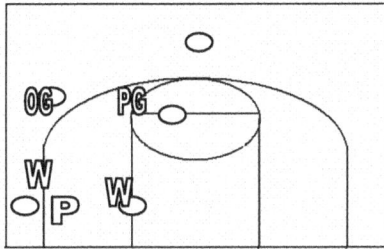

DIAG 49

Conclusion

I hope that this gives you and your team a solid starting place should you decide to implement the 1-1-3. Below are a few of the key teaching point that I feel you need to remember in this process,

- Emphasize solid man principles.
- Make your post work the post arc to keep from getting pinned.
- Backside wings must play up the lane.
- Stress Communication.
- Rotation, Rotation, Rotation.

Always remember that there is more than one way to skin a cat. Take what we have given you and always work to improve the system. Even today seven years after we began this experiment we are always making adjustments and improvements. With that said I wish you the very best of luck in your future with the match-up zone.

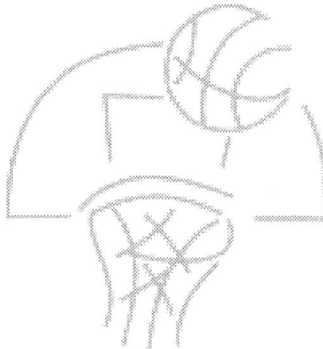

About the Author

Jason Montgomery is a veteran of fourteen years of coaching in both the prep and collegiate ranks and has found success wherever he has gone. Currently he is the Head Coach at Nature Coast Technical High School in Brooksville, Florida where he has led the Lady Sharks to three consecutive twenty win seasons as well three appearances in the state sweet sixteen.

Prior to his current stint at Nature Coast, Jason spent five seasons at Saint Catharine College, three as head coach, where he also posted back to back twenty win seasons. His collegiate teams were renowned for their aggressive defensive style and up-tempo offense. In all five seasons while on staff, Saint Catharine finished the season ranked in the top fifteen in the nation in points per game and in his final season at the helm the team set the school record posting 137 points in a win over conference rival Jackson State.

Coach Montgomery's success has not gone unnoticed. Montgomery has now been honored as "coach of the year" a total of ten times including twice being selected as a Florida Athletic Coaches Association regional "coach of the year" and state finalist.

Individual recognition has also been plentiful for Montgomery's players as he has coached four conference player of the year selections, two area players of the year, two all-Americans and numerous all conference and all area selections. This success has not come with a sacrifice in the classroom either. Montgomery's teams have been honored nationally for their academic success and while at Saint Catharine College he held a 100% graduation or matriculation rate for players that stayed with the program for two years.

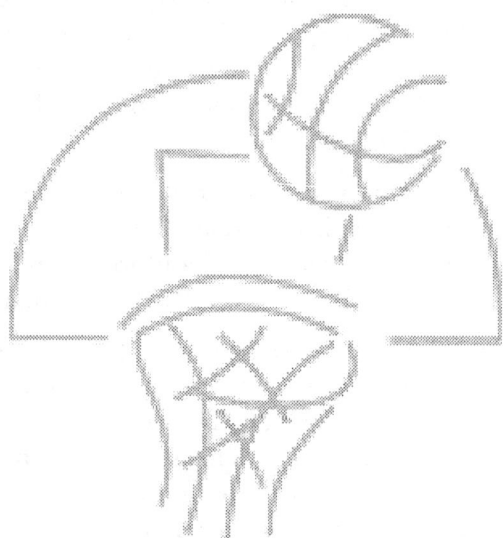

NOTES:

NOTES:

NOTES:

NOTES:

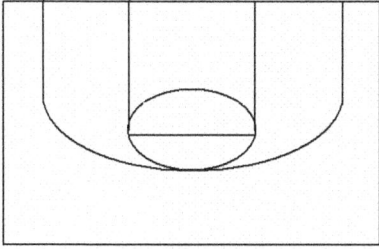
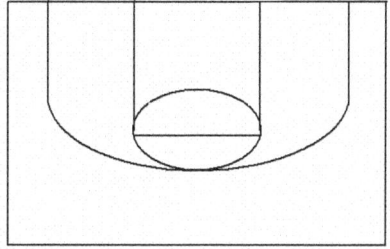

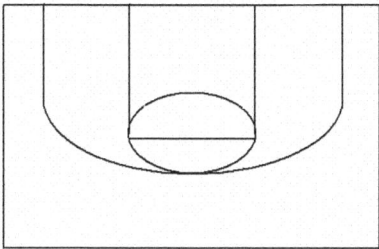
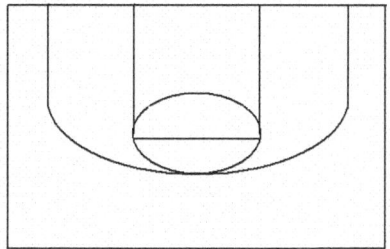

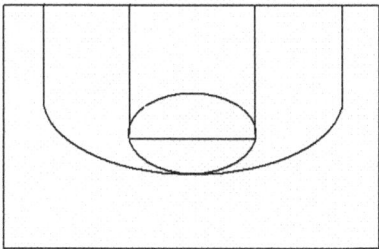
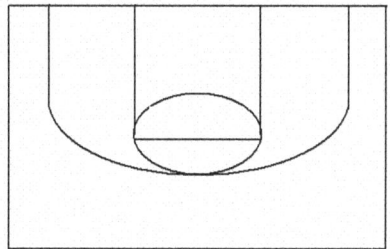

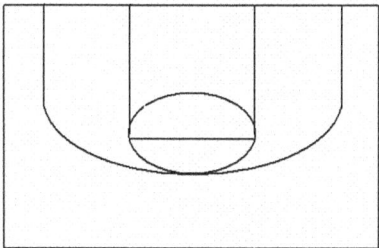
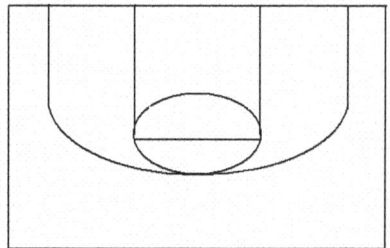

The Definitive Guide to the 1-1-3 Match-up Zone

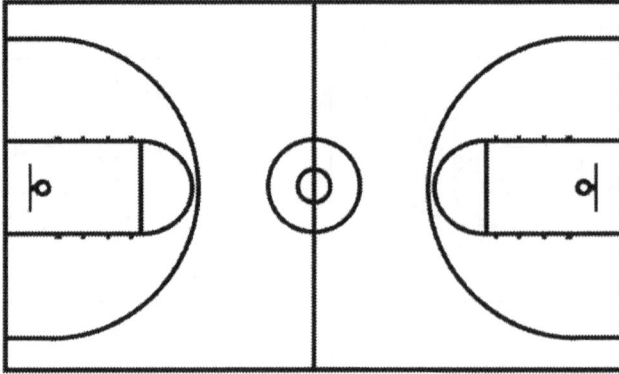

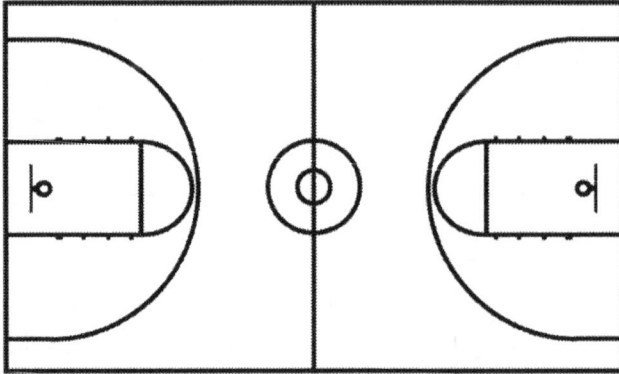

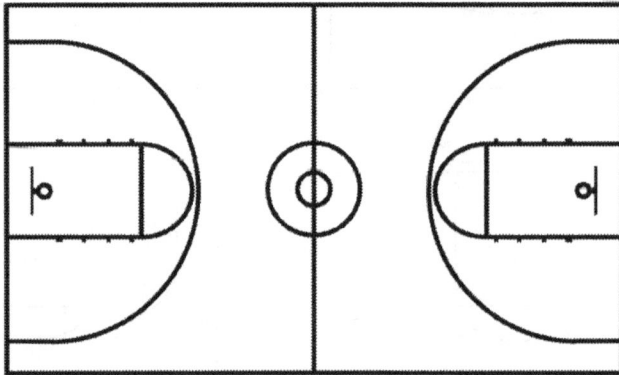

The Definitive Guide to the 1-1-3 Match-up Zone

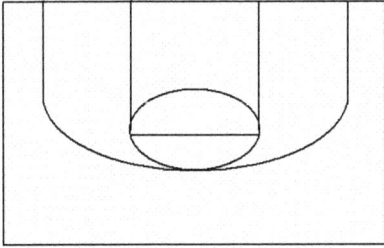
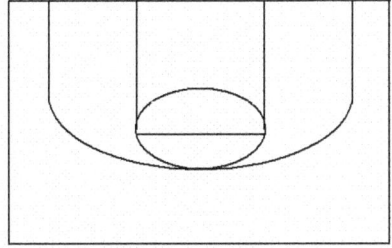

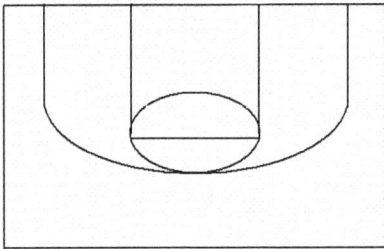
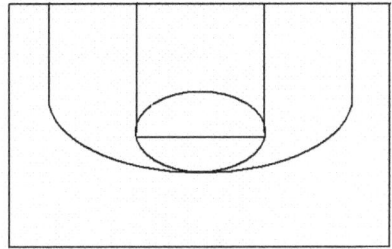

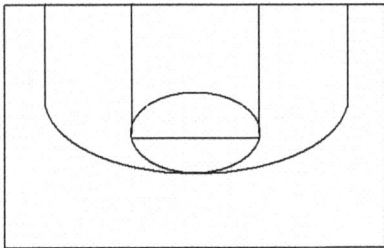
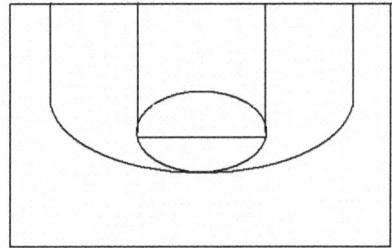

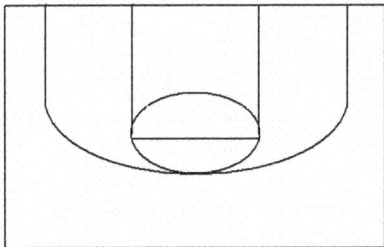
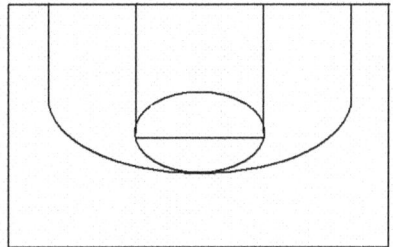

The Definitive Guide to the 1-1-3 Match-up Zone

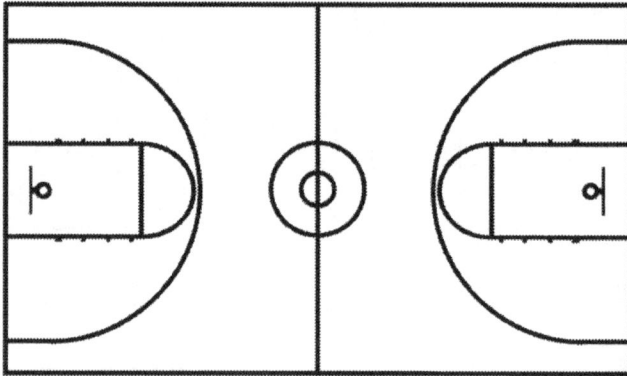

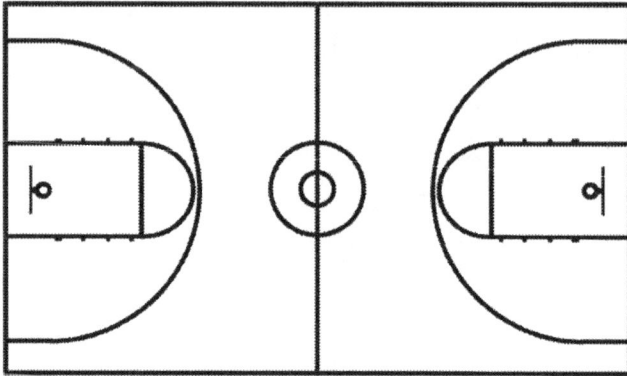

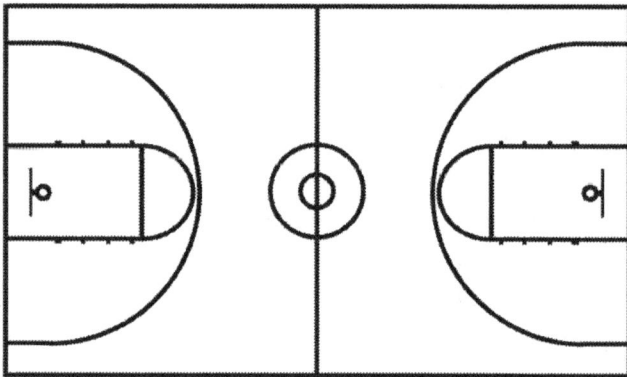

The Definitive Guide to the 1-1-3 Match-up Zone

www.ingramcontent.com/pod-product-compliance
Lightning Source LLC
LaVergne TN
LVHW091211080426
835509LV00006B/939